ABOARD HMS BEAGLE

BY TANYA DELLACCIO

 Gareth Stevens
PUBLISHING

Please visit our website, www.garethstevens.com. For a free color catalog of all our high-quality books, call toll free 1-800-542-2595 or fax 1-877-542-2596.

Library of Congress Cataloging-in-Publication Data

Names: Dellaccio, Tanya, author.
Title: Aboard HMS beagle / Tanya Dellaccio.
Description: New York : Gareth Stevens Publishing, [2020] | Series: History
   on the high seas | Includes index.
Identifiers: LCCN 2018059653| ISBN 9781538237861 (paperback) | ISBN
   9781538237885 (library bound) | ISBN 9781538237878 (6 pack)
Subjects: LCSH: Beagle (Ship)–Juvenile literature. | Beagle Expedition
   (1831-1836)–Juvenile literature. | Darwin, Charles, 1809-1882–Juvenile
   literature. | Natural history–Juvenile literature. | Evolution–Juvenile
   literature.
Classification: LCC QH11 .D45 2020 | DDC 576.8/2-dc23
LC record available at https://lccn.loc.gov/2018059653

First Edition

Published in 2020 by
Gareth Stevens Publishing
111 East 14th Street, Suite 349
New York, NY 10003

Copyright © 2020 Gareth Stevens Publishing

Designer: Katelyn E. Reynolds
Editor: Therese M. Shea

Photo credits: Cover, p. 1 SCIENCE PHOTO LIBRARY/Getty Images; cover, pp. 1–24 (porthole and wood background) Andrey_Kuzmin/Shutterstock.com; cover, pp. 1–24 (wood sign) ESB Professional/Shutterstock.com; cover, pp. 1–24 (brass plate) photocell/Shutterstock.com; pp. 2–24 (old paper) Kostenko Maxim/Shutterstock.com; pp. 4–24 (old notebook) BrAt82/Shutterstock.com; p. 5 (main) The Print Collector/Getty Images; p. 5 (inset) Jdcollins13/Wikipedia.org; p. 7 Bettmann/Getty Images; pp. 9 (main), 13 (inset) DEA PICTURE LIBRARY/De Agostini/Getty Images; pp. 9 (inset), 17 (main) Peter Hermes Furian/Shutterstock.com; p. 11 Sémhur/Wikipedia.org; p. 13 (main) DeA/Icas94/De Agostini/ Getty Images; p. 15 Dorling Kindersley/Getty Images; p. 17 (inset) Scewing/Wikipedia.org; p. 19 Print Collector/ Hulton Fine Art Collection/Getty Images; p. 21 John Arrowsmith/Hesperian/Wikipedia.org.

Printed in the United States of America

CPSIA compliance information: Batch #CS19GS: For further information contact Gareth Stevens, New York, New York at 1-800-542-2595.

CONTENTS

WORDS IN THE GLOSSARY APPEAR IN **BOLD** TYPE THE FIRST TIME
THEY ARE USED IN THE TEXT.

INTO THE UNKNOWN

Much of what we know about the world today was once a mystery. Over the years, people have spent a lot of time, money, and effort trying to better understand Earth and its **geography**.

Before modern **technology** was available, the best way to make a map of unknown lands was by ship. Many voyages, or journeys, were planned for this purpose. In the 1800s, the ship called HMS *Beagle* took part in several **surveying** voyages. It became known because of the discoveries it made possible.

CREWMAN'S LOG

In this log, or record, you'll read more about the voyages of the HMS Beagle from a sailor's viewpoint. These writings are fictional, or made up, but they're based on facts.

SCIENTIST CHARLES DARWIN, A TRAVELER ON ONE OF THE *BEAGLE'S* VOYAGES, BECAME FAMOUS FOR HIS OBSERVATIONS ABOUT PLANTS, ANIMALS, AND EVEN PEOPLE!

Charles Darwin

5

ALL ABOARD!

There were nine British naval vessels, or ships, with the name *Beagle* at different times. After one *Beagle* was no longer used, a new naval vessel could adopt this name.

The most well-known *Beagle* was the third one. It was a ship made for scouting and similar duties, not war. Still, it had 10 cannons on board! The vessel was changed a bit over the years, depending on its **mission**. It completed three voyages in all.

CREWMAN'S LOG

It's an honor to serve on the *Beagle*! Some think it's strange to name a ship after a kind of dog, but a few British ships have been named for animals. "HMS" stands for: His (or Her) Majesty's Ship.

THE THIRD HMS *BEAGLE* WAS **LAUNCHED** IN 1820 AT THE BRITISH NAVY'S SHIPYARDS ON THE RIVER THAMES NEAR LONDON, ENGLAND. ITS FIRST MISSION WASN'T UNTIL 1826.

7

TO SOUTH AMERICA

The first voyage of the third HMS *Beagle* began on May 22, 1826. The crew's mission was to help the HMS *Adventure* survey the areas at the southern end of South America called Patagonia and Tierra del Fuego. Lieutenant Pringle Stokes was the *Beagle*'s captain at first. After his death on the voyage, Lieutenant Robert Fitzroy took over as captain. Fitzroy found a channel passable by ship through the islands of Tierra del Fuego. He named it the Beagle Channel. The vessel returned to England in 1830.

CREWMAN'S LOG

We're on a hydrographic surveying mission. The captain said these fancy words mean we gather facts about water depth, the shape of the sea floor and coast, and other features in and around the water.

TIERRA DEL FUEGO IS AN ARCHIPELAGO, OR A GROUP OF ISLANDS, AT THE SOUTHERN TIP OF SOUTH AMERICA. *TIERRA DEL FUEGO* IS SPANISH FOR "LAND OF FIRE." THIS PAINTING SHOWS NATIVES OF TIERRA DEL FUEGO WAVING AT THE HMS *BEAGLE*.

SOUTH AMERICA

Patagonia

Tierra del Fuego

Beagle Channel

9

SECOND TIME AROUND

The HMS *Beagle* departed, or set off, on its second voyage on December 27, 1831. The journey was supposed to take 2 years, but the crew ended up spending almost 5 years away from home!

The voyage continued the first mission. The crew would gather information, or facts, about lands surrounding South America. The information would be used to create better maps for the British government. Much more happened on the journey, however. The trip would become world-famous.

CREWMAN'S LOG

We're getting ready to depart on the Beagle. It's going to be a long and hard journey, but I think I'll be back with my family in 2 years. Captain F. told us it might be a little longer!

HMS BEAGLE'S SECOND VOYAGE

North America

Europe

Asia

Africa

South America

Australia

Antarctica

ON ITS SECOND VOYAGE, THE HMS *BEAGLE* TRAVELED TO SOUTH AMERICA AND
THEN WENT ON TO CIRCUMNAVIGATE, OR SAIL AROUND, THE WORLD.

CLOSE QUARTERS

For the second voyage, the HMS *Beagle*'s captain was again Robert Fitzroy. He was also a **meteorologist**. Fitzroy's job was to command the voyage, keeping the crew on track to complete their mission.

The crew numbered around 70 men, but the ship had little space to hold them all. The HMS *Beagle* was only about 90 feet (27 m) long, which didn't leave much room for the crew's living quarters. Scientific tools of the day were also important **cargo**.

CREWMAN'S LOG

One tool that I use a lot is the chronometer. It helps me keep track of the time so that I can measure **longitude** better. That means I know where we are on a map!

ONE INSTRUMENT FOUND ON THE HMS *BEAGLE* WAS A THEODOLITE, WHICH IS A TELESCOPE-LIKE TOOL THAT MEASURES ANGLES. IT'S USEFUL FOR SURVEYING.

Robert Fitzroy

13

A SPECIAL SAILOR

Being a captain on a long journey was lonely, hard work, and it was hoped that another scientist would make a good companion for Captain Fitzroy. Fitzroy heard about 22-year-old naturalist Charles Darwin and invited him on the voyage.

Darwin had a big mission, too. As a naturalist, he studied living things and the **environments** in which they lived. His task on the voyage was to explore and collect **specimens**. He spent much of his time exploring on land.

CREWMAN'S LOG

It's probably for the best that Darwin is on land so much. When he does stay on the ship, he sleeps in a **hammock** just 2 feet (61 cm) from the ceiling!

IN THE 5 YEARS THAT THE *BEAGLE* WAS AT SEA, DARWIN SPENT ONLY ABOUT 18 MONTHS ABOARD.

Charles Darwin

On his travels, Darwin found many fossils, which are marks or remains of plants and animals that formed over thousands or millions of years. He also found a lot of skulls and skins from different animals. He began to study them and wonder what makes some species, or kinds, of animals die out.

Darwin studied living things, too. On the Galápagos Islands, off South America, he collected samples of small birds from different islands. Today, they're known as Darwin's finches. These birds helped him form a **theory**.

CREWMAN'S LOG

Darwin keeps collecting things and bringing them back on the ship. We're running out of room! He told me he's written 1,750 pages of notes on all the different things he's found.

16

A BIG DISCOVERY

Darwin's finches led him to his theory of natural selection. He noticed that the birds were very similar—except for their beaks. Each had a beak perfect for the food in its environment. He concluded that the beaks had evolved, or changed over time, for the species to survive.

Darwin continued to build on this theory. He came to the conclusion that people, like animals, have evolved. He wrote several books on his findings after the *Beagle* returned in October 1836.

CREWMAN'S LOG

I think Darwin may have stumbled upon something amazing. What if, like the finches, humans adapted to their surroundings? I think there's a much larger meaning to all of this!

DARWIN'S FINCHES

GEOSPIZA MAGNIROSTRIS

*Known as the large ground-finch.
Beak adapted to eat large,
hard seeds from the ground.*

GEOSPIZA FORTIS

*Known as the medium ground-finch.
Beak adapted to eat seeds of
all sizes from the ground.*

CAMARHYNCHUS PARVULUS

*Known as the small tree-finch. Beak adapted
to pick small bugs and leaves off bark,
and to bite through twigs and stems.*

CERTHIDEA OLIVACEA

*Known as the warbler finch.
Beak adapted to eat small insects.*

NATURAL SELECTION IS THE WAY BY WHICH PLANTS AND ANIMALS ADAPT, OR CHANGE, TO BETTER FIT THEIR ENVIRONMENT. THEY PASS ON ADAPTATIONS TO THEIR BABIES. THOSE THAT CANNOT ADAPT DO NOT SURVIVE. DARWIN'S FINCHES OFFERED PROOF OF THIS THEORY.

AUSTRALIA AND BEYOND

The third voyage of the HMS *Beagle*, from 1837 to 1843, explored territory in Australia. The crew named a port after Charles Darwin and a river after Robert Fitzroy. That was this *Beagle's* last voyage.

However, the *Beagle* had accomplished a lot. It had helped people discover more about Earth's geography and aided in the creation of new maps. It had also transported the naturalist Charles Darwin to the locations that led to his important theory. The *Beagle* helped change people's understanding of the natural world forever!

CREWMAN'S LOG

I served on the Beagle until 1843. After that, she was used as a place to watch for **smugglers**. She was renamed, sold, and finally broken into pieces. How sad! What a wonderful ship she was!

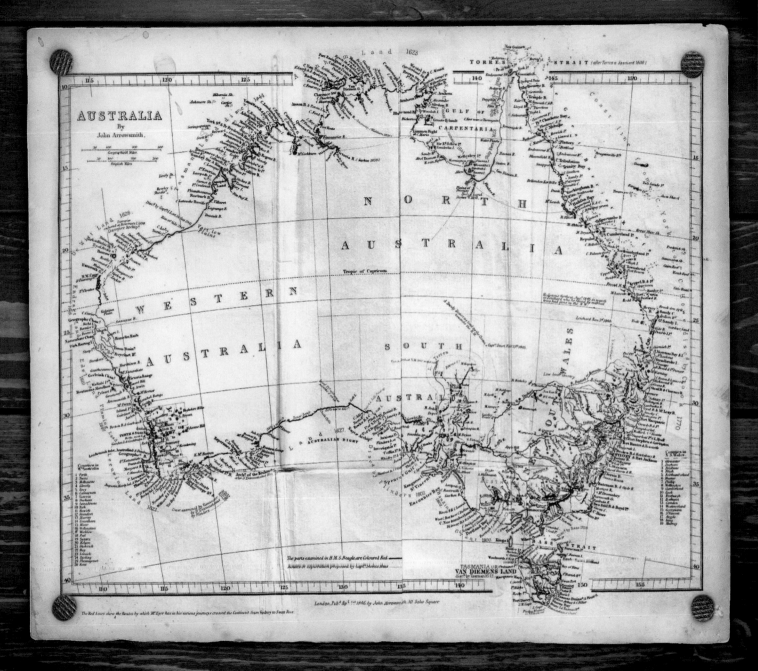

THE PARTS OF AUSTRALIA EXPLORED BY THE HMS *BEAGLE*
ARE HIGHLIGHTED IN RED.

21

GLOSSARY

cargo: goods carried by a plane, train, truck, or boat

environment: the conditions that surround a living thing and affect the way it lives

geography: the study of Earth and its features

hammock: a type of bed that consists of a piece of cloth hung between two places

launch: to put a ship on the water

longitude: the imaginary lines that run north and south to the east and west of the prime meridian

meteorologist: someone who studies weather, climate, and the atmosphere

mission: a task or job a group must perform

smuggler: one who moves something from one country to another illegally and secretly

specimen: a sample of a group

surveying: having to do with measuring land areas

technology: the way people do something using tools and the tools that they use

theory: an explanation based on facts that is generally accepted by scientists

FOR MORE INFORMATION

Books

Coates, Eileen S. *Charles Darwin and the Origin of Species.* New York, NY: PowerKids Press, 2019.

Morlock, Theresa. *HMS Beagle Voyage and the Galápagos Islands.* New York, NY: PowerKids Press, 2019.

Stine, Megan. *Where Are the Galápagos Islands?* New York, NY: Grosset & Dunlap, 2017.

Websites

HMS Beagle
www.projectbritain.com/calendar/May/beagle.html
Find more information about the HMS *Beagle* and its most famous voyage.

Who Was Charles Darwin Video for Kids
easyscienceforkids.com/who-was-charles-darwin-video-for-kids/
Learn more about Charles Darwin with a video and short biography on his life.

INDEX